Piano for Adults

Level One Method
by Wesley Schaum

Teacher Consultants: Alfred Cahn, Joan Cupp, Sue Pennington

Index

EXCLUSIVELY DISTRIBUTED BY

HAL•LEONARD®
CORPORATION
7777 W. BLUEMOUND RD. P.O. BOX 13819 MILWAUKEE, WI 53213

ISBN-13: 978-1-62906-034-7

01-51

Foreword

This method is tailored for an older individual – adult or teenager. It may also be used for mature students of a younger age.

The progress here is <u>much more gradual than other adult methods</u>. This allows the student to be entirely comfortable with the learning steps. The rate of progress is flexible; work in this book can be leisurely or fast paced, depending upon the individual pupil and preference of the teacher.

The musical excerpts are themes from symhonies, operas, ballets, concertos, oratorios, chamber music, vocal and choral literature. Also included are folk songs from many ethnic groups. No simplified piano music is used. Music appreciation stories, biographical information and portraits of the composers are provided.

A <u>minimum of finger numbers</u> are used. Various changed and extended hand positions are used to avoid becoming locked into a rigid five-finger position. Simple transposing is featured. Chord symbols are incorporated for some accompaniments.

Emphasis is placed on recognition of repeated patterns in melody and accompaniment, along with analysis of simple musical form. This knowledge provides significant help in reading music, learning pieces and memorizing.

A reference page, correlating notes and keyboard position along with basic musical symbols, is found on the front inside cover and continued on the back inside cover. A <u>music dictionary</u>, appropriate for level one, is provided on pages 46-47. The <u>index</u> on page 48 helps to locate explanations contained within the method.

Musicianship Curriculum

Sound musicianship is attained by thorough musical study, and staying on each level until it is mastered. It is intended that this method book be part of a systematic approach to learning to play the piano. This done by working in four books at the same level before moving up to the next level.

1. Method   2. Theory   3. Technic   4. Repertoire

This 4-book curriculum may be tailored to each individual student, depending on age, ability and interests. Here are some of the Schaum supplements available at this level. At least one book should be assigned in each category, with preference to the first title in each group.

Theory Books:
Theory Workbook, Level 1
Composer Note Speller
Keynote Speller, Level 1
Rhythm Workbook, Level 1

Technic Books:
Fingerpower®, Level 1
Fingerpower® Etudes, Level 1
Fingerpower® FUN, Level 1
Masters of Technic, Level 1

Repertoire Books & Sheet Music:
see our website for a complete listing of all Level 1 materials – www.schaumpiano.net

Contents

Instrument Care and Maintenance

Acoustic Piano

General Care: An acoustic piano is made with hundreds of small mechanical parts and should be treated with respect. Children should not be allowed to pound on the keys, sit on the keyboard or put their full weight on the pedals. Care should be taken to avoid spilling any liquid onto the keyboard and to prevent small objects, such as coins, pins or paper clips from falling into the spaces between the keys. The top lid of an upright piano should be kept closed to prevent unwanted objects from falling inside. Special caution is needed for a grand piano, since the lid is usually left partly open.

The piano should be treated like any other piece of fine furniture. Liquids can be particularly harmful. Overflow from watering plants and condensation from beverage containers should be promptly wiped up so as not to damage the finish. Pianos with a high-gloss finish may be dulled with ordinary furniture polish or pre-treated dust cloths. Check the manufacturer's instructions for care of the finish on your instrument.

Keyboard: Prior to 1946, ivory was used for the white keys of pianos. Today, white plastic is used instead. Both ivory and plastic keys may be cleaned with a soft, damp cloth and mild soap. Be careful to avoid excess water in the cleaning rag. Don't use cleaners that will leave an oily residue on the keys, since it may make them slippery or sticky. Window glass cleaner is good for most plastic keys.

Environment: Humidity and temperature play a significant role in the stability of tuning and the mechanical operation of a piano. To avoid wide fluctuations, don't place the piano in front of a window, radiator or heating duct, or where it will be exposed to direct sunlight. If possible, avoid placing the piano on an outside wall. A piano should not be placed in a basement, unless it is dry and an electric dehumidifier is used.

The winter and summer seasons bring unavoidable changes in humidity and temperature which cause the instrument to go out of tune. When heat is turned on during the fall and winter, humidity drops and the pitch of a piano will drop slightly. During the spring and summer, when humidity rises, the pitch also rises slightly. Unfortunately, such changes of pitch are not uniform and the result is an uneven shift of the tuning. If a piano is not tuned for several years, this seasonal process of uneven shifting back and forth makes the piano sound progressively worse.

Tuning: Every piano has 200 or more strings, each fastened with its own tuning pin. When a piano is tuned, each of the pins must be adjusted with a special socket wrench. Don't try this yourself, because it's easy to pull a string too tight and break it.

A piano dealer or your piano teacher can provide the name of a reliable tuner/technician. It is best to employ a tuner who is a registered member of the Piano Technicians Guild. Information is available on the internet.

A professional technician will need 1½ to 2½ hours to tune a piano. During this time it should be as quiet as possible. Therefore, household members should be prepared to go without the TV or stereo, and noisy activities should be avoided.

It is desirable to have a piano tuned once or twice each year. The best time is to schedule it when the temperature and humidity are expected to be reasonably stable for three to four months; for example, 4 to 6 weeks after the heating or cooling season has started.

If your piano has not been tuned for a long time and is badly out of tune, the technician may recommend several tunings to bring the pitch up to normal. Occasionally, a string may break in the process of tuning, especially with older instruments. This can usually be replaced immediately, but the new strings require several "touch-up" tunings to stabilize the pitch.

If problems exist such as sticky keys, squeaky pedals, or strange noises, the tuner is usually able to repair these in your home. Be sure to tell the tuner in advance, so extra time can be scheduled. Obtain a cost estimate before giving your consent for the repair. Some repairs require taking part of the piano to the technician's shop. Always get a written estimate before proceeding with work outside your home. If the cost seems excessive, get a second opinion from another technician.

Digital Piano • Electronic Piano • Electronic Keyboard

General Care: Electronic instruments, like the piano, require the same respectful use of the keyboard, and prevention of small objects from getting between the keys. Place the instrument to avoid flucuations in temperature and humidity. Avoiding direct sunlight is particularly important. Follow the manufacturer's instructions regarding cleaning of exposed surfaces.

Special Precautions: Spilled liquids can be a disaster for an electronic instrument. Every key on the keyboard has electrical contacts and /or electronic sensors. Various controls and electronic components, installed behind the keyboard, are also vulnerable. NEVER put plants, beverages, food or any liquid container on an electronic instrument. Components damaged by liquids are very expensive to replace. Electronic instruments are especially susceptible to damage from bumping and rough treatment. They should be moved carefully and handled to avoid accidental dropping.

It's advisable to protect your electronic instrument with a "surge protector," the same as is recommended for computer equipment. It's also a good idea to disconect the power cord from the wall receptacle if you are going to be away from home, or the instrument will not be used for several days.

If your instrument has a compartment for batteries, check at least every three months for battery leakage. If batteries are seldom used or not needed, it's better to remove them completely.

Tuning: Electronic or digital pianos and electronic keyboards never need tuning, however, most instruments have a small knob or control for making slight changes in pitch, which may accidentally be moved, causing the pitch to be higher or lower than normal. This control is usually on the back of the instrument and often inconspicuous. Consult the manufacturer's instructions for the location and proper setting of the tuning control. (This is NOT the same as the control used for transposing.)

Melodic Interval Refresher
An *interval* is the distance in sound between one note and another.
The *interval number* is the same as the number of *alphabet letters* it includes, as shown in the line below.

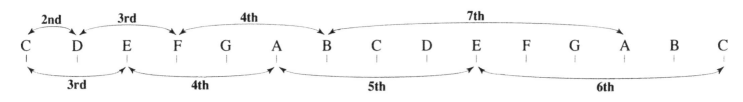

Preparatory: Count and tap the rhythm to the treble clef notes below. Keep your counting very steady and even.
   The first note, in an incomplete measure, is a *pick-up* or *up-beat* note.
   The counts missing at the beginning of this piece are balanced by the final measure.

On Wings of Song (Mendelssohn, Op.34, No.2)

Directions: This piece includes many things presented previously in the beginner level. If you have any questions, use the reference page (front inside cover), the music dictionary on page 46, or the index on page 48.

Counting numbers are printed between staffs. Finger numbers are printed above or below the note.

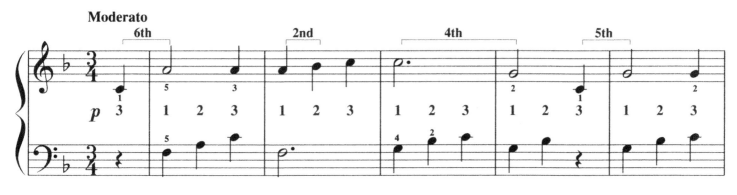

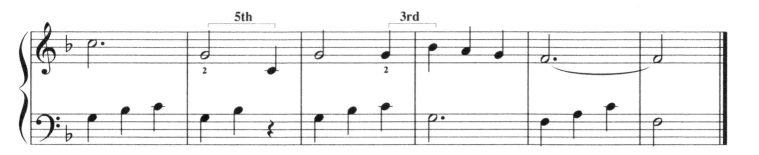

Felix Mendelssohn (MEN-dell-sohn) • 1809-1847 • Germany
Mendelssohn was very well known throughout Europe as a conductor and composer, although he was also an accomplished pianist and organist. As a conductor, he worked to improve the quality of orchestral performances, and broadened musical appreciation by introducing a wide variety of composers and soloists. He wrote symphonies, overtures, concertos, piano pieces, vocal, choral and chamber music. This song is one of set of six, written between 1834 and 1836.
   He was an admirer of the works of Bach and Mozart. At the time, Bach was considered very old-fashioned and his music almost forgotten. Mendelssohn's efforts aroused new interest and appreciation of Bach's music.

Phrase Marks and Ties

A *phrase mark* is a curved line placed over or under groups of notes indicating the length of a *phrase*. A phrase is a musical sentence, and often coincides with punctuation in the lyrics. Notes within the phrase are to be played *legato*. The last note of a phrase should be released slightly early to create a small gap between phrases. Phrase marks are labeled in the music below.

Performance of a phrase is more easily illustrated by singing the melody and taking a short breath at the end of each phrase, but *without interrupting the rhythm*. This creates a small gap in the sound between phrases. A similar effect is desirable at the keyboard.

A TIE is also a curved line, but connects notes on the *same line or space* that are *next to each other*. Ties are labeled in the music below.

Flowers That Bloom in the Spring from "The Mikado" (Gilbert & Sullivan)

Directions: If necessary, practice hands separately first. In the first measure of the 2nd line of music, notice that the melody alternates between right and left hands. The same alternation recurs toward the end. After the piece is learned, try singing the melody and taking a short breath at the end of each phrase, as described in the second paragraph above. Try to imitate this *breath* at the keyboard by releasing the last note of each phrase a little early.

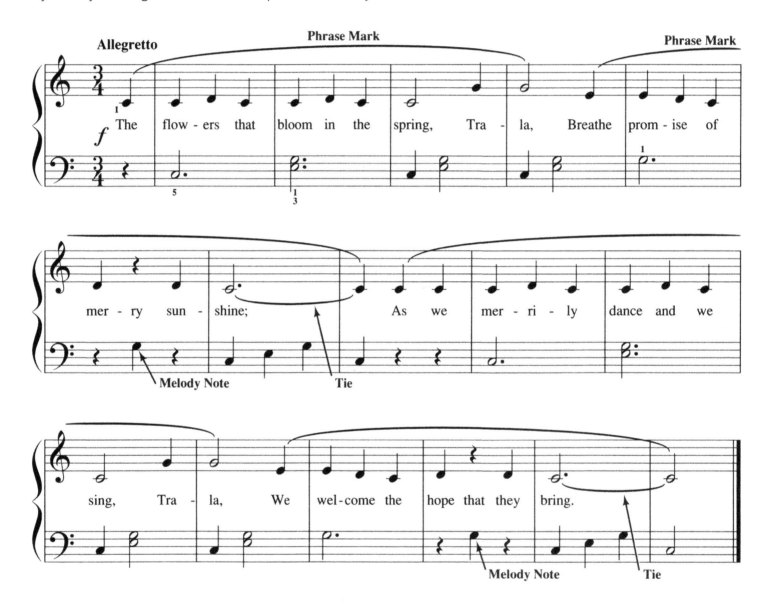

Sir Arthur Sullivan (SULL-ih-vun) • 1842-1900 • England
During his lifetime, Sullivan was England's most famous composer. He is best known for the comic operas written with W.S. Gilbert. Sullivan wrote music to fit Gilbert's lyrics. Their productions enjoyed enormous popularity. For example, "The Mikado" ran for 672 performances beginning in 1885. Sullivan also wrote several hymn tunes including, "Onward Christian Soldiers."

Gilbert and Sullivan's comic operas are delightful satires of late 19th century English aristocracy, social customs, legal system and government bureaucracy. The "Mikado" is one of the best known. The story is set in Japan (the Mikado is the emperor) and involves a ridiculously entangled love story that is resolved by preposterous events.

New Notes: Treble D and E
The new notes, D and E, are shown in the sample staff at the right. Refer to the front reference page to find their position on a keyboard diagram.

Musette from "Armide" (Gluck)

Directions: If necessary, practice hands separately at first. Watch for fingering changes in the right hand. Also look for repeated patterns in the bass clef.

A *dissonance* occurs each time the note G# is played. The dissonance is resolved on the next count.

Christopher Willibald Gluck (GLOOK) • 1714-1787 • Germany
Gluck was an important composer in the development of opera as we know it today. He was one of the first to tailor the music to fit the mood and meaning of the lyrics and also the dramatic implications of the opera story. "Armide" was written in 1777.

Gluck was a successful opera composer in both Paris and Vienna. Marie Antoinette, queen of France, took voice and harpsichord lessons from him for several years. He wrote over forty operas, music for several ballets plus vocal music. Some of his works were commissioned by the royal family of Austria.

Schaum's **Theory Workbook, Level 1** provides written work coordinated with this book to reinforce the learning elements.

New Note: Leger Line D

The sample staff shows new bass notes, D and D-flat, on a leger line. These are played with the left hand.

Lonesome Road (African-American Folk Song)

Directions: As a preparatory, count and tap the rhythm for the treble staff notes of this piece. Watch for changes of hand position in *both hands*. After the solo part can be played comfortably,

1. Sing the words while playing, for ear training and vocal development.
2. Have your teacher play the duet accompaniment.

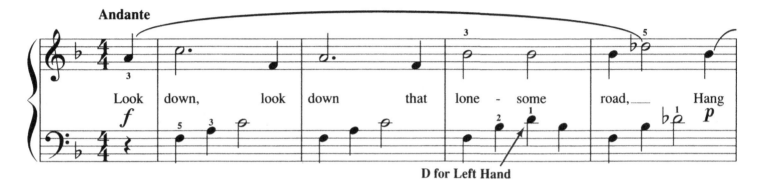

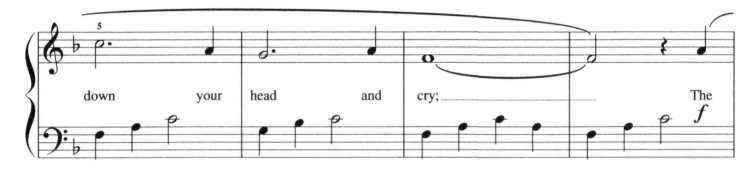

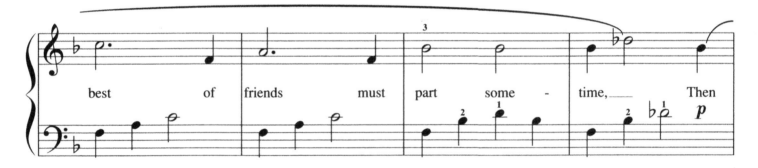

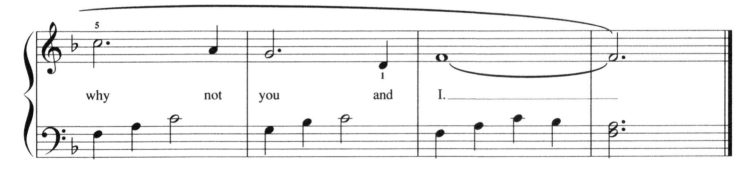

DUET ACCOMPANIMENT
Stem Down = Left Hand — Stem Up = Right Hand

Left Hand Melody and Cross Over
The melody for this piece is played entirely by the left hand.

Roses From the South   (Strauss)

Directions: As a preparatory, play the entire left hand part alone. When playing the right hand accompaniment, *listen carefully*. The right hand notes must be played softer <u>so the melody can be heard clearly</u>. Be sure to observe the rests by releasing the key for the duration of each rest.

The left hand should *cross over the right hand* when playing the treble clef C, in the last measure.

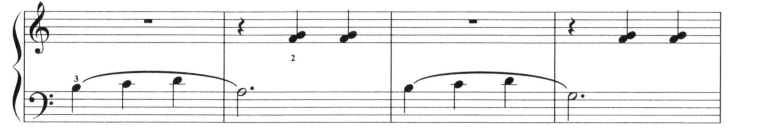

L. H. Cross Over

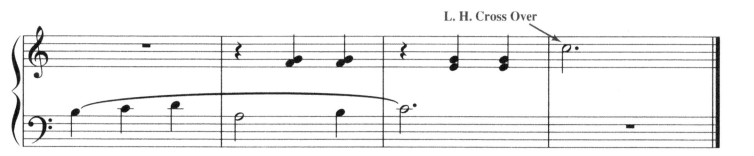

DUET ACCOMPANIMENT

10

Crescendo and Diminuendo

Crescendo (cre-SHEN-doh) is an Italian word meaning to gradually <u>increase</u> the loudness (abbreviated **cresc.**)
The piece below starts **p**, meaning soft. Beginning at *cresc.*, you are to gradually increase the loudness so that by the middle of the 2nd line of music you are playing **f**, meaning loud.

Diminuendo (di-min-you-END-oh), also Italian, means to gradually <u>decrease</u> the loudness (abbreviated **dim.**)
In the 3rd line of music you should be playing **f**. Beginning at *dim.*, you are to gradually decrease the loudness so that in the final measure you are playing **p**.
   Diminuendo does NOT mean to go slower or change the tempo.

Theme from 7th Symphony (Beethoven, Op.92, 2nd Movement)

Directions: As a preparatory, count and tap the treble clef rhythm for the first line. Counting numbers are printed between the staffs. Notice the staccato dots that go with all of the 8th notes. At first, work on playing the correct notes and rhythm. Then, observe the *cresc.* and *dim.* marks, as explained above.

Ludwig Van Beethoven (BAY-toe-ven) • 1770-1827 • Germany
Beethoven's musical innovations have influenced many other important composers, including Schubert, Mendelssohn, Wagner, Brahms and Dvorak. Beethoven spent most of his life in Vienna, Austria where his music enjoyed continuous popularity since it was introduced.
   The 5th Symphony was first performed in 1808 and the 7th Symphony in 1813. In addition to nine symphonies, Beethoven wrote 32 piano sonatas (each one ranging from 8 to 54 pages long), numerous pieces of chamber music (see below) as well as one opera and much choral and vocal music.

Chamber music is written for a group of two to ten players perfroming in a small hall or recital room. Varous combinations of string, woodwind and brass instruments are used, often with piano. The most common chamber groups are the duet, trio and quartet.

Schaum's Fingerpower®, Level One provides basic technic exercises to strengthen fingers and develop dexterity.

Fortissimo – Importance of Listening

$\boldsymbol{ff}$ Abbreviation of **fortissimo** (fohr-TISS-ee-moh), an Italian word meaning very loud.

It is very important that you <u>LISTEN as you play</u> and train your ear to recognize different levels of loudness. This should be coordinated with training your sense of TOUCH to recognize the *feeling* needed in the fingers and hands.

Theme from 5th Symphony   (Beethoven, Op.67, 1st Movement)

Directions: As a preparatory, count and tap the treble clef rhythm. The counting is shown between the staffs. Notice that the first beat at the beginning is a REST. Watch for changes of fingering, especially in the right hand. Various melodic intervals are indicated with brackets (refer to page 5).

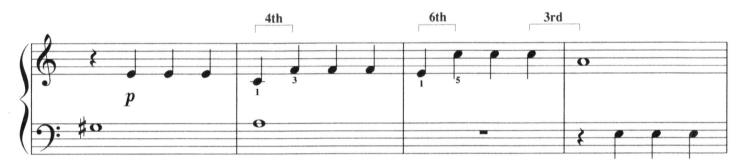

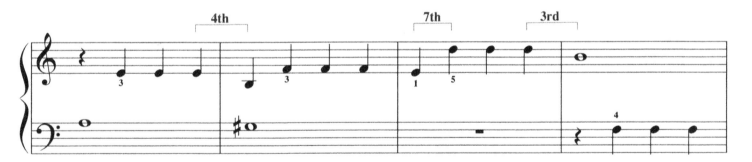

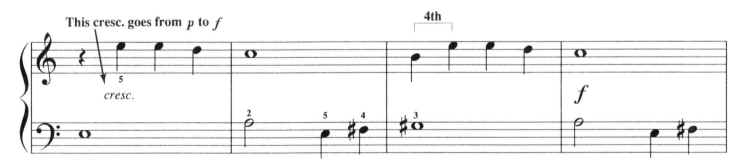

12

Half Steps and Whole Steps

A **half step** is the distance from one key to the *closest* black or white key. There is <u>no key in between</u>. Sometimes a half step is from one white key to the next white key. Various half steps are labeled on the keyboard diagrams below. Half steps may go up or down.

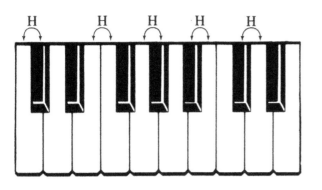 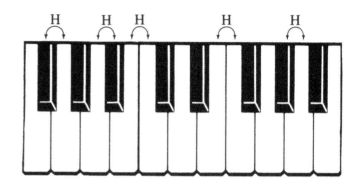

A **whole step** always <u>skips one key</u>, which may be black or white. Whole steps may go up or down. Different whole steps are labeled on the diagrams below.

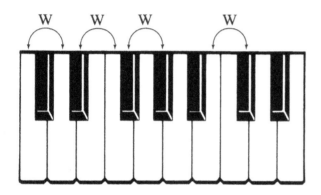 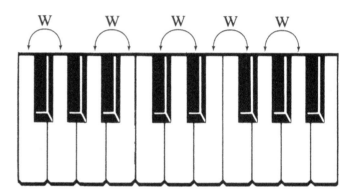

Directions: Compare the two notes in each measure below. Write the letter H (= Half step) or the letter W (= Whole step) on the dotted line below each measure. If necessary, refer to the keyboard diagrams above. It is NOT intended that these two lines be played. They are for written work only.

Half Step Melody (Schaum)

Directions: The right hand notes consist entirely of *half steps* (see page 12) except for one interval. Can you find it?
Notice that some of the black keys are spelled in two different ways.

Whole Step Melody (Schaum)

Directions: The right hand and left hand intervals consist entirely of *whole steps* (see page 12).
This results in some dissonance and unusual sounds called *whole tone harmony*.

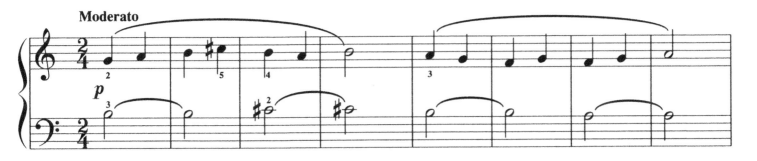

14

Transposing to Black Keys - Sharps

To *transpose* means to play in a different key. In the music below, the same melody appears in the key of F major and then is transposed to black keys, all sharps.

Key of F major: **Lil' Liza Jane** (American Folk Song)

Directions: The key signature of one flat (B flat) is required for F major, even though this piece does not have any B's.

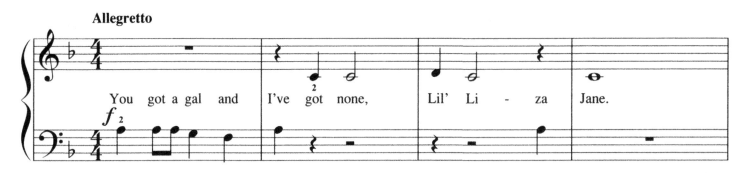

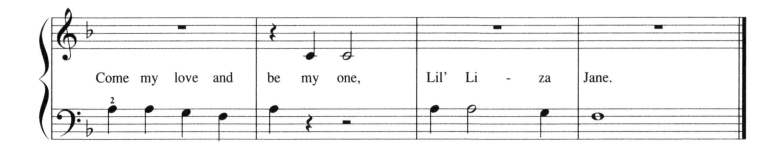

Black Keys, Sharps: **Lil' Liza Jane** (American Folk Song)

Directions: This version is played entirely on black keys. It uses the same fingering and counting as in F major, above. The note positions in the staff are the same, but all notes are sharp.

When transposing upward by making all notes sharp, you are raising the melody by one **half-step**. For more information about half steps, see page 12.

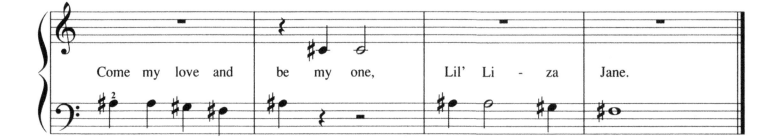

Transposing to Black Keys - Flats

In the music below, the same melody appears in the key of G major and then is transposed to black keys, all flats.

When transposing downward by making all notes flat, you are lowering the melody by one **half-step**. For more information about half steps, see page 12.

Key of G major: **Lil' Liza Jane** (American Folk Song)

Directions: The key signature of one sharp (F sharp) is required for G major, even though this piece does not have any F's. The fingering is the same as both versions on page 14.

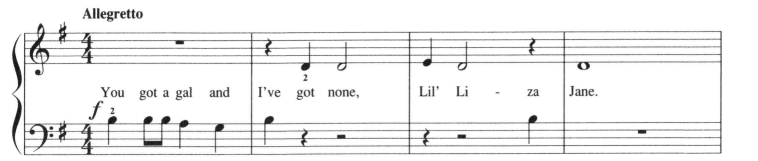

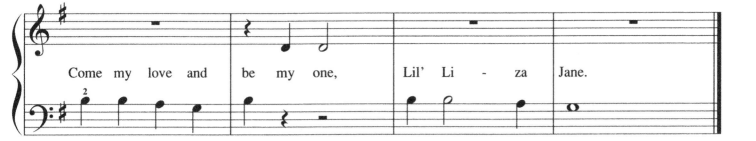

Black Keys, Flats: **Lil' Liza Jane** (American Folk Song)

Directions: This version is played entirely on black keys. It uses the same fingering and counting as in G major, above. The note positions in the staff are the same, but all notes are flat.

Notice that the black key melody here *sounds the same* as the black key melody on page 14. This illlustrates <u>two different names for each black key</u>. For example, F-sharp and G-flat are two names for the *same black key*.

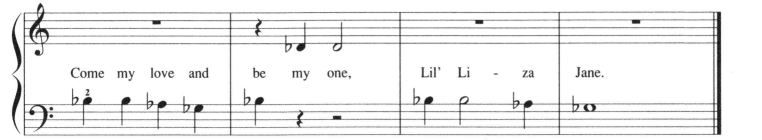

16

Major Scale Construction

A major scale is a pattern of *whole steps* and *half steps* in musical alphabet order. The eight notes of the major scale have number names called **degrees**.

The keyboard diagram shows the C Major Scale with *degree numbers* printed on the keys. The two *half steps* are indicated with the letter H. All other steps are *whole steps*.

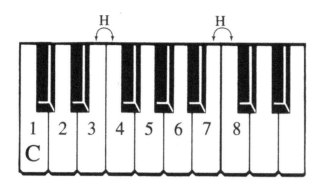

Every major scale has TWO HALF STEPS. They are always:
between the **3rd and 4th** degrees and between the **7th and 8th** degrees.

All other steps are *whole steps*.

The 8th degree has the *same letter name* as the 1st degree, but is *one octave* higher.

The degrees of the scale are similar to the steps of a ladder. The illustration shows the sequence of whole steps and half steps in a major scale.

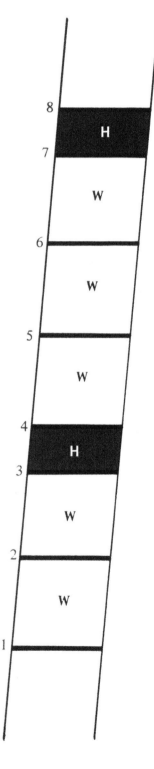

Directions: The keyboard diagram below shows the **F major scale**. The degree numbers are printed on the keys. Draw arrows and write the letter H between the proper degrees to indicate the *half steps* (similar to the example at the top of this page).

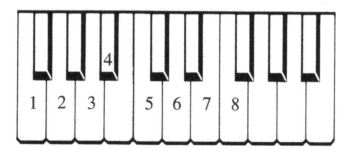

Directions: The keyboard diagram below shows the **G major scale**. The degree numbers are printed on the keys. Draw arrows and write the letter H between the proper degrees to indicate the *half steps* (similar to the example at the top of this page).

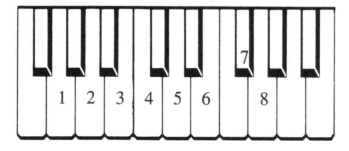

C Major Scale and Thumb Crossings

Playing of scales involves special movements of the thumb to play the notes *legato*. The thumb may be crossed *underneath* the fingers or fingers may be crossed *over* the thumb.

These thumb and finger crossings are essential because many pieces require similar fingering maneuvers. See "Leschetizky's Practice Stunt" at the bottom of this page.

C Major Scale – Right Hand

Directions: Watch the finger numbers carefully. Be sure to play all notes of the scale *legato*. Practice the scale slowly at first and gradually increase the tempo as it gets more comfortable.

C Major Scale – Left Hand

Directions: Watch the finger numbers carefully. Be sure to play all notes of the scale *legato*. Practice the scale slowly at first and gradually increase the tempo as it gets more comfortable.

F Major Scale

Directions: This scale is divided between hands. Watch the key signature. The larger numbers are *scale degree numbers*.

G Major Scale

Directions: This scale is divided between hands. Watch the key signature. The larger numbers are *scale degree numbers*.

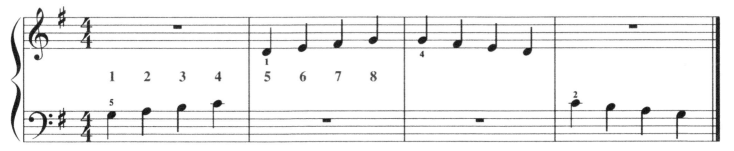

Leschetizky's Practice Stunt

Leschetizky (Lesh-ih-TISS-key) was a famous concert pianist and teacher born in Poland (1830-1915). It is said that he had his pupils practice with a coin on the back of each hand. If the hand and wrist were kept steady as the thumb was passed under, the coin would not fall off while playing and Leschetizky was satisfied with the hand position.

Play the C major scale, on hand at a time this way, but use a large coin (quarter or bigger), so it doesn't fall into the cracks between the piano keys. A large button or a bottle cap may be used instead.

Teacher's Note: Tetrachord fingering, divided between hands, is used here for the the F major and G major scales because the student has not yet learned the full range of notes in the staff. These scales, with all notes in one hand, will be presented at the next level.

Thumb Crossings

Crossing the thumb <u>under</u> fingers or crossing fingers <u>over</u> the thumb, as used in scale playing, is often encountered in music.

The Heavens Are Telling from "The Creation" (Haydn)

Directions: The right hand has several thumb crossings indicated by arrows. Portions of a scale (scale passage) are found in two places in the melody. Although they do not begin on G, they use the notes of the G major scale (page 17).

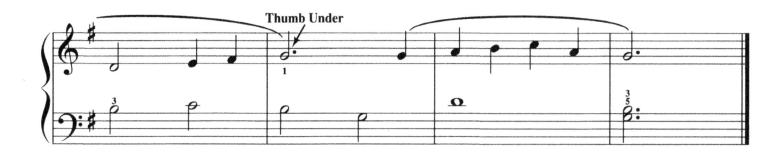

Franz Joseph Haydn (HIGH-den) • 1732-1809 • Germany

"The Creation" was first performed in Vienna in 1798 and is Haydn's most famous oratorio. It relates the Biblical story of the creation of earth. It uses vocal soloists, choir and a small orchestra. "The Creation" is often performed in large churches or in concert halls. Haydn wrote five other oratorios.

Among Haydn's numerous works is a hymn tune that became the national anthems of both Austria and Germany. Many American churches use the same music for the hymn "Glorious Things of Thee Are Spoken."

Suggested repertoire book with music appreciation stories and pictures: Schaum's *Classic Melodies from Great Symphonies*.

Extension Dots and Staccato Dots

A dot along the SIDE of a note head makes the note value *longer*. It is called an *extension* dot.

A dot ABOVE or BELOW the note head means to play with a short, quick-release touch. It is called a *staccato* dot. It does NOT change the value of the note.

Jarabe Tapatio ("Mexican Hat Dance") (Mexican Folk Song)

Directions: As a preparatory, count and tap the treble clef rhythm for the first two lines of music. Notice that the rhythm for the remaining lines is the same, except for the final note. Counting numbers are printed between the staffs.

There is a scale passage in the final two measures. Watch for the thumb crossing under. Also look for various extension dots and staccato dots.

Key Signature: B-flat Major

The *two flats* used in the key signature for *B-flat Major* mean that <u>all B's and E's are flat</u>. A key signature eliminates the need to write a flat sign for every B and E.

B-flat and F7 Chords - New Note: Bass B-flat

Two new chord patterns are shown here. Notice that the broken chord pattern extends over two measures. The new bass note, B-flat, is used in one of the chords. Refer to the keyboard chart on the front inside cover, if necessary.

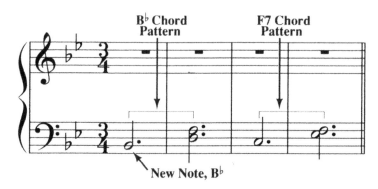

Rig-A-Jig-Jig (English Folk Song)

Directions: Be sure to play all B's and E's *flat* as indicated in the key signature. Watch the finger numbers carefully, especially for the black keys.

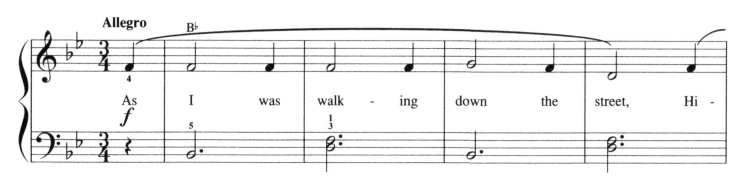

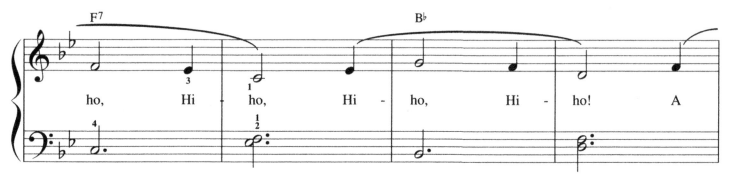

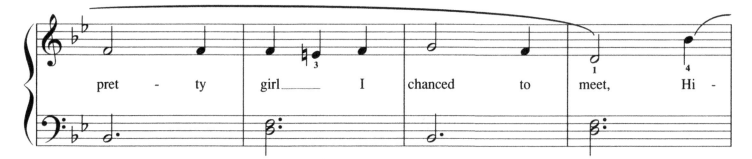

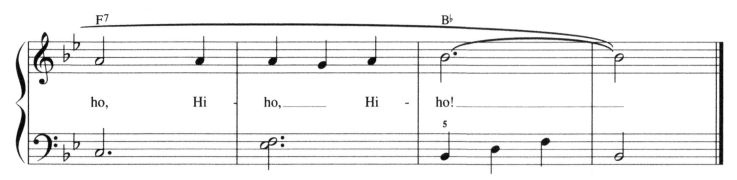

Teachers Note: It is not intended that root position and inversions be explained here. The slash sign, used to indicate the bass note in a chord symbol, therefore, is not used. Various inversions and other chord symbols will be presented later in this series.

E-flat Chord

The E-flat chord is shown here with the left hand fingering and chord symbol.

Aloha Oe (Queen Liliuokalani)*

Directions: As a preparatory, play the entire bass clef part alone. Notice that the B-flat and F7 chords are used (see page 20) but with a different rhythm. Watch for changes of fingering in the right hand.

DUET ACCOMPANIMENT

* Queen Liliuokalani (lee-lee-OO-oh-kah-LAH-nee) was the last reigning monarch of Hawaii before annexation to the United States. She lived from 1838 to 1917. Her reign as Queen was from 1891 to 1893. "Aloha Oe" is probably the best known piece of music written by a native Hawaiian.

Blocked Chords – G and D7 Chords

When all notes of a chord are played simultaneously, it is called a *blocked chord*. The sample measures show the G chord and D7 chord in two versions, as a *broken* chord and a *blocked* chord.

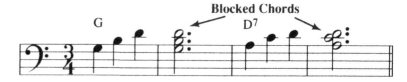

Cockels and Mussels (Irish Folk Song)*

Directions: As a preparatory, play the entire bass clef part alone. In the accompaniment, the G chord is played first as a broken chord, then as a blocked chord. The D7 chord is then played the same way.

Be careful to play all three notes of each blocked chord so they sound <u>at precisely the same time</u>. It would be good to practice this piece very slowly at first, gradually increasing the tempo until the chords can be played fluently.

The first note in the left hand is a melody note, after that, the left hand notes should be played softer so the right hand melody may be heard clearly. The left hand also has one melody note at the end of the second line of music.

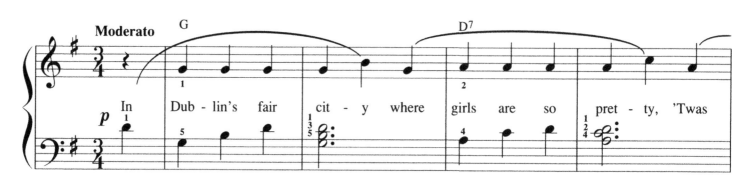

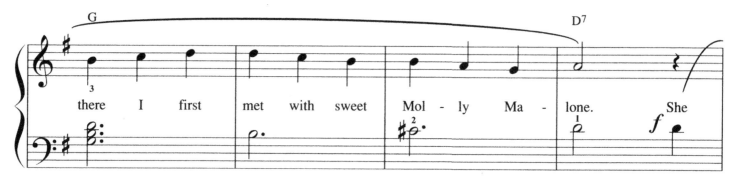

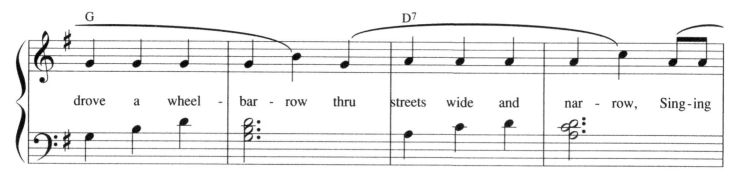

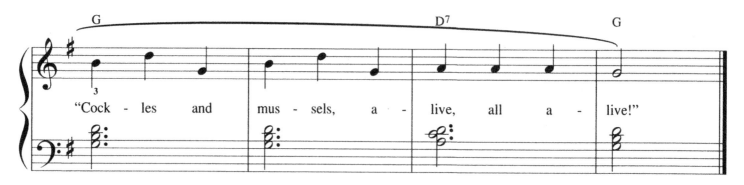

* The lyrics describe a street vendor in Dublin, the capital city of Ireland. Cockles and mussels are edible shellfish, varieties of the clam. They can be dug out of the sand near the water on many ocean beaches.

More Blocked Chords – F minor Chord

The sample measures show the three blocked chords used in this piece, along with their fingering.
The chord symbol for <u>F minor</u> has a small letter "m" next the letter "F". The chord includes a black key.

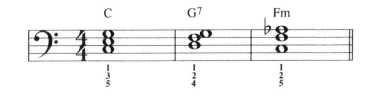

O Solo Mio (di Capua)*

Directions: As a preparatory, play the entire bass clef part alone. In the accompaniment, you will find a mixture of broken chords and blocked chords. Be sure that the three notes of each blocked chord are played simultaneously.

* This music, written in 1898, is one of the most famous of all Italian songs. Although di Capua wrote other ballads, none have achieved the status of this one. Eduardo di Capua was born in Naples, Italy and lived from 1864 to 1917.

A **ballad** (BAL-id) is a sentimental or romantic song which tells a story, often with descriptive music and several verses.

F Chord

The sample measures show the F chord as a broken chord and as a blocked chord.

Notice that the chord symbol is slightly different than for the F *minor* chord on page 23.

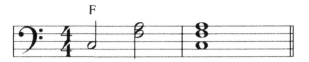

Allelujah from "Exsultate, jubilate" (Mozart, K165)*

Directions: As a preparatory, play the entire bass clef part alone. The broken chords and blocked chords are similar to those on page 23. Be careful that the three notes of each blocked chord are played *precisely at the same time.*

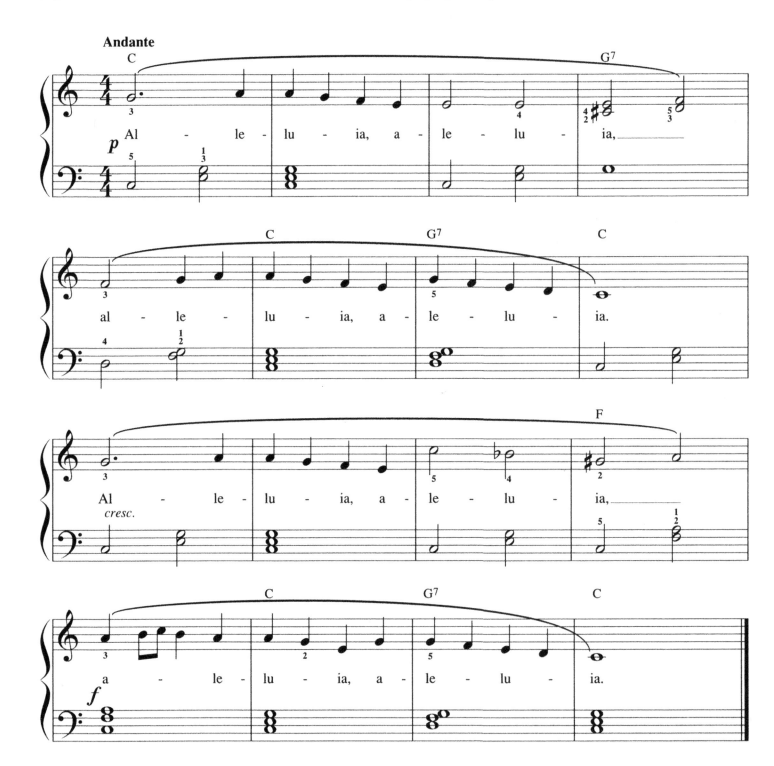

* A **motet** (moh-TET) is a piece of choral music usually based on a religious text and intended for a church service. Mozart, however, wrote this motet for soprano solo with instrumental accompaniment. This well-known theme is from the motet, "Exsultate, jubilate," written in 1773. Although Mozart wrote only four motets, he wrote much other music for the church.

Melody Changing Hands – Accent Mark

It is important to identify the location of the melody, which sometimes changes from one hand to the other. Some of the bass clef notes are marked with a short horizontal line called an **accent mark**. The accent points out the left hand melody notes and serves as a reminder that the melody should be played slightly louder than the accompaniment.

Accidentals as Reminders

Many composers and editors, especially in student editions, add extra accidentals which are not really necessary. Although a bar line always cancels any accidentals used in a previoius measure, extra accidentals may be used as a reminder. These are labeled in the music below. Such accidentals are sometimes enclosed in parentheses.

Waltz from "Sleeping Beauty"   **(Tchaikowsky, Op.66)***

Directions: The melody begins in the left hand and changes to right hand in the third line of music. It switches back to the left hand in the last line. Bass clef melody notes are indicated with accent marks.

   The key signature for B-flat major is two flats. Be sure to play all B's and E's flat.

Watch for the left hand crossing over into treble clef in the final measure.

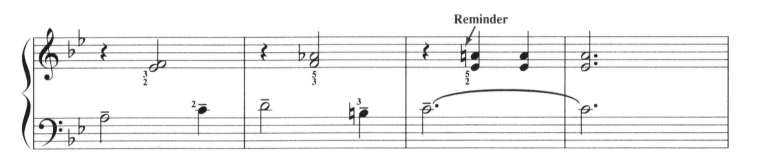

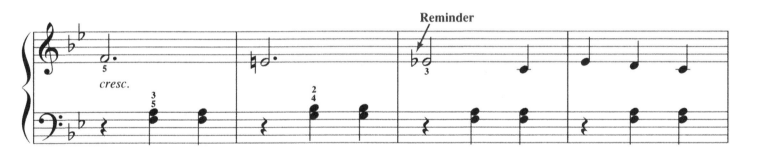

* The ballet, "Sleeping Beauty," was first performed in 1890 in St. Petersburg, Russia. Tchaikowsky considered it one of his best compositions. It uses the familiar fable of a princess cursed by a wicked fairy. After sleeping 100 years. the princess is awakened by a kiss from Prince Charming. The two are married in an elaborate wedding ceremony. Tchaikowsky wrote three ballets, "Sleeping Beauty," "Swan Lake," and the "Nutcracker," all of which are regularly performed by American ballet companies.

Mezzo-Forte and Mezzo-Piano

mf = Abbreviation of **mezzo-forte** (MET-zoh FOHR-tay), an Italian word meaning <u>medium loud</u>.

mp = Abbreviation of **mezzo-piano** (MET-zoh pee-YAA-noh), an Italian word meaning <u>medium soft</u>.

Notice that *p* is <u>softer</u> than *mp*. Remember that *f* is <u>louder</u> than *mf*.

Angel Fair With Golden Hair (Liszt)

Directions: As a preparatory, play the entire bass clef part. Notice that the accompaniment in the second line is the same as the first line. The accompaniment in the third line has only one note different that the first two lines. <u>Can you find it?</u>

Watch the dynamics carefully. Each line is to be a little louder than the line before.

Franz Liszt (LIST) • 1811-1886 • Hungary

Liszt was the most famous concert pianist in all of Europe during his time. He gave recitals beginning at age 11, and by age 20 had appeared many times in Ireland, England, France, Germany, Portugal, Russia and Turkey, as well as other European countries. He had unusually large hands which enabled him to play and compose extremely difficult music.

In addition to a large amount of piano music, he wrote orchestral music, sacred vocal music, songs and many transcriptions using themes of other composers. A **transcription** usually makes a piece of music more elaborate and difficult than the original version. This song was written in 1839.

Rehearsal Numbers

The circled numbers in measures 5, 9, and 13 are called *rehearsal numbers*. The same numbers also appear in the duet accompaniment. They are for convenience when practicing the duet.

She'll Be Comin' 'Round the Mountain (American Folk Song)

Directions: This piece has a 2/4 time signature. If there is a question about the counting, see page 10.
Watch for changes of fingering in the right hand.

This piece should be practiced slowly at first. If necessary, play hands separately. Be careful that the notes and rhythm are correct as the tempo is gradually increased.

DUET ACCOMPANIMENT

28

Key Signature: D Major
The *two sharps* used in the key signature for *D Major* mean that
<u>all F's and C's are sharp</u>. The key signature eliminates the need to
write a sharp sign for every F and C.

Scheherazade (Rimsky-Korsakov, Op.35)

Directions: Be sure to play all F's and C's *sharp* as indicated in the key signature. Watch the finger numbers carefully,
especially for the black keys.

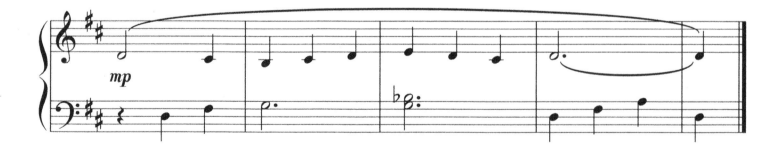

Nikolay Rimsky-Korsakov (RIM-skee CORE-sah-kov) • 1844-1908 • Russia
Rimsky-Korsakov was a composer and professor at the St. Petersburg Conservatory. His teaching influenced
many important Russian composers. He wrote a textbook on **orchestration**, which is the combination and
interaction of various instruments in a musical composition. He is best known for his operas and orchestral
music.
   Queen Scheherazade (shah-hair-ah-ZAHD) is the make-believe story-teller of the tales of the Arabian
Nights. This theme is from an orchestral suite written in 1888.

Country Gardens (English Folk Dance)

Directions: As a preparatory, play the treble clef part for the entire piece. Watch for the 3rd finger crossing over, as shown in the first line. Be sure to play all F's and C's *sharp* as indicated by the key signature.

Notice that the melody in the first, second and fourth lines is the same. However, finger numbers are found only in the first line. Where the notes are the same, whether melody or accompaniment, the fingering is also the same.

DUET ACCOMPANIMENT

Symbols for Crescendo and Diminuendo

is a symbol for **Crescendo** which means to gradually <u>increase</u> the loudness. (See page 10.)

is a symbol for **Diminuendo** which means to gradually <u>decrease</u> the loudness. (See page 10.)

Because these symbols are similar, study them carefully. They are both like the letter V turned sideways and stretched out. The "point" of the V is always softer.

Heavenly Aida from "Aida" (Verdi)

Directions: Watch for symbols for *crescendo* and *diminuendo* used in this piece.
The right hand has several places where the thumb crosses under. Watch the fingering carefully.

DUET ACCOMPANIMENT

Giuseppe Verdi (joo-SEHP-ee VAIR-dee) • 1813-1901 • Italy
Verdi is one of the best-loved of all opera composers. He wrote 28 operas, "Aida" (Ah-EE-dah) being one of the most famous. Commissioned for the new opera house in Cairo, Egypt, its first performance there in 1871 was an overwhelming success. "Aida" is a grandiose production with elaborate settings and costumes.

Aida is an Ethiopian princess loved by Rhadames, commander of the Egyptian army opposing the Ethiopians. Their love causes Rhadames to betray his country. He condemned to death and Aida chooses to die with him. "Heavenly Aida" is from Act 1, Scene 1.

Octave Higher Sign

The number 8 (sometimes **8va)**, followed by a broken line and placed <u>above</u> a series of notes, is called an *octave higher sign*. The notes in the first staff beneath the broken line are to be played <u>one octave higher than written</u>. This applies only to the notes in one staff. In this piece, only the treble clef notes are affected.

The same sign, when placed <u>below</u> the notes, means to play one octave lower than written. An example is in the final measure of the duet accompaniment on this page. The octave lower sign may also be **8vb**.

Passepied from "Le Roi s'amuse" (Delibes)

Directions: This piece uses the same melody two times. The second time it is played one octave higher. The accompaniment is the same each time. In this piece, the bass clef notes are NOT affected by the octave higher sign.

The intervals in the accompaniment are labeled in the first four measures. These same intervals are used in the remainder of the piece. For more information about intervals, see page 5.

DUET ACCOMPANIMENT

Leo Delibes (dah-LEEB) • 1836-1891 • France

Delibes is best known for his ballets "Coppelia" and "Sylvia," which are both regularly performed by American ballet companies. Delibes also wrote one other ballet and over 20 operettas and comic operas. "Le Roi s'amuse" (the king's amusement) is a series of six orchestral dances written in 1882 for a Victor Hugo play.

The **passepied** (pahs-pee-YAA) is a French court dance popular during the 17th and 18th centuries. It was also used in ballets and instrumental music.

Common Time

The symbol **C** is sometimes used as a substitue for a 4/4 time signature. Notes are counted in the same manner with either time signature. It is called "common time" because 4/4 is found so often in music.

Melody Patterns

Many pieces contain sections of melody that are repeated. On this page, the first three measures of lines 1, 2, and 4 are the same, as indicated with brackets. The accompaniment for these measures is also the same.

Looking closer, the entire 2nd line and 4th line are the same, except for one added accompaniment note in the final measure. Looking for melody patterns helps in learning and memorizing music.

On the Bridge at Avignon (French Folk Song)

Directions: The bass clef accompaniment has intervals of a 2nd and 3rd as indicated in the first two measures. These same intervals are used again later in the music. <u>Can you find them?</u>

Sometimes the lyrics of a piece are printed separately, like a poem. In this piece, each line of the lyrics fits with a phrase of music. Try writing the lyrics in the music, fittting the syllables with notes as needed.

On the bridge, on the bridge,
On the bridge at Avignon.
On the bridge, on the bridge,
People dancing all around.

Gentlemen go this way.
All the ladies that way.
On the bridge, on the bridge,
On the bridge at Avignon.

Transposing

The music on this page is a transposed version of the piece in the key of F major on page 32. The same melody and accompaniment are written here except everything is now in the key of G major.

All notes on this page are *one whole step higher* than on page 32. (See page 12 for an explanation of whole steps.)

On the Bridge at Avignon (French Folk Song)*

Directions: Compare the music on this page with page 32. Notice that the intervals of the melody, from one note to the next, are the same on both pages. The intervals of the accompaniment notes have the same relationship.

The left hand fingering is the same on both pages. The right hand fingering is the same except for measures 8 and 16. The melody patterns and intervals pointed out on page 32 also appear in this G major version.

* Avignon is a town in southern France with a rich musical and cultural heritage dating back to the early 1300's. The St. Benezet Bridge is an ancient stone structure crossing the Rhone River. Avignon is currently home to an opera company, a summer music festival and one the largest chamber music societies in France.

Song of the Volga Boatmen (Russian Folk Song)*

Directions: Accent marks (see page 25) are used as a reminder showing where the melody is in the bass clef. Be sure to listen carefully and play the accompaniment softer than the melody.

Watch for places where the melody changes from one hand to another.

* For many years before the development of steam engines, barges loaded with produce and freight were hauled between towns along the Volga River, one of the principal rivers in Russia. Teams of men tugging together on heavy ropes pulled each barge from along the river bank. This "work song," sung as the men toiled, helped to pass the time and promote teamwork. The minor key and slow pace of the music reflects their laborious task.

There Stands a Little Man from "Hansel and Gretel" (Humperdinck)

Directions: This piece has several bass clef melody notes indicated with accents. It also uses some *staccato* notes (see page 19).

Engelbert Humperdinck (HUM-purr-dink) • 1854-1921 • Germany
Humperdinck is best known for his opera, "Hansel and Gretel," first produced in 1893. It was so successful that it was produced at fifty theaters during its first year. It started as home entertainment for his family and eventually grew to be a full length opera. The **libretto** (story-text and lyrics) was written by Humperdinck's sister and is based on one of the well-known Grimm fairy tales. The music is charming, melodious and skillfully orchestrated. Humperdinck also wrote other operas, incidental music for four Shakespearean plays, choral and vocal music.

The lyrics for the piece "There Stands a Little Man," are in the form of a riddle. The answer to the riddle is "a mushroom."

During the 1960's, an American pop singer assumed the stage name, Engelbert Humperdinck, presumably because he thought it quaint and unique. He has no relationship to the German opera composer.

D and A7 Chords

The D and A7 chords are shown with their chord symbols in the sample measures.

New Leger Note: A

The sample measure shows the note "A" written on the second leger line below the treble staff. It is to be played with the right hand. It is the same key as the bass clef note "A" shown beside it.

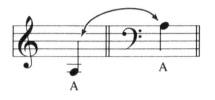

Goodbye Old Paint (American Cowboy Song)*

Directions: The key signature for D major is two sharps. Be sure to <u>play all F's and C's sharp</u>. Watch for the new leger note "A" below the treble staff. It is used in the 8th measure.

The A7 chord is used in two different ways in the accompaniment (measure 3 and measure 15). The notes are the same, but the broken chord pattern changes in measure 15.

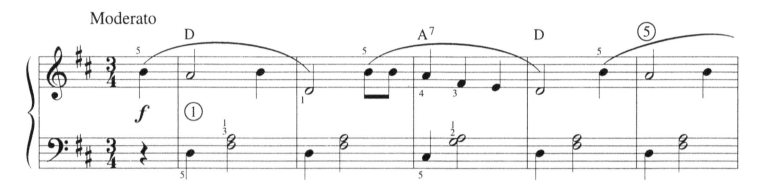

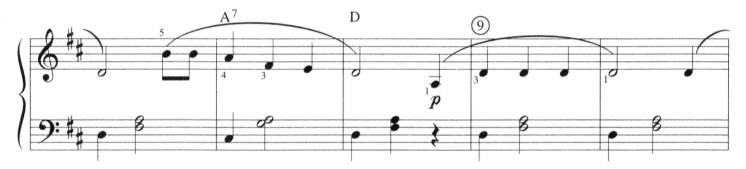

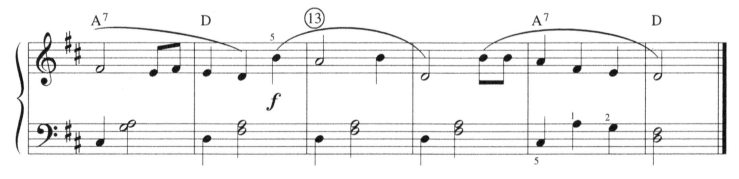

DUET ACCOMPANIMENT

* "Old Paint" is the name of a cowboy's horse.

Inversions of Chords

To invert a chord means to regroup the notes. A 3-note chord can have two inversions. The G major chord is shown in its **root position** (with G at the bottom) and in two inversions. Notice that when moving from root position, the note is taken off the bottom and put on top, as shown by the arrows.

New Bass Notes: G and B

The two lowest notes in the root position G chord are shown here. Find their keyboard position on the front reference page.

Double Tie

A tie may connect more that two notes, as shown in measures 6-7-8 and in measures 14-15-16. The key is to be held down continuously for the combined value of all the notes tied together.

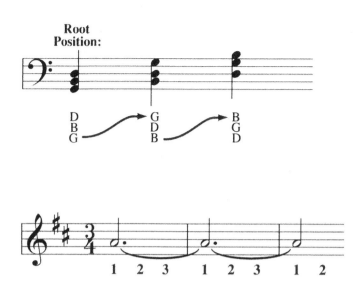

On Top of Old Smoky (American Folk Song)

Directions: This piece is in the key of D major. Be sure to play all F's and C's sharp.

The root position of the G major chord is found in measures 2 and 3. Watch for the new notes G and B. Inversions of the G chord are found in measure 4 and in measure 15.

The D chord and A7 chords are found as broken chord accompaniments using different rhythm patterns. Symbols for crescendo and diminuendo are found here (see page 30).

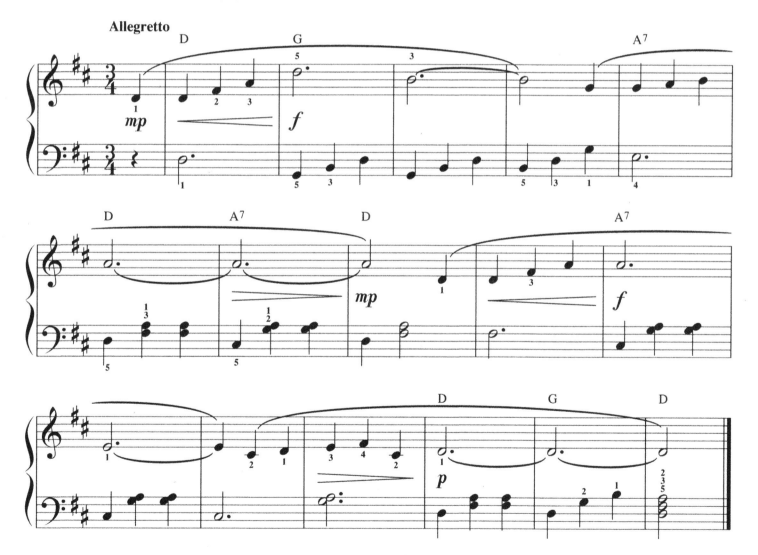

On top of old Smoky,	A-courtin's a pleasure,	A thief, he will rob you
All covered with snow,	A-flirtin's a grief,	And take what you have,
I lost my true lover,	A false-hearted lover,	A false-hearted lover,
Come a-courtin' too slow.	Is worse than a thief.	Will send you to your grave.

Memorizing

To memorize a piece of music means to play it without the printed music. Careful dailiy practice lays a foundation for memorizing. Unfortunately, mistakes are easily memorized. Therefore, practicing the correct notes and rhythm, using proper fingering, and observing dynamics and phrasing are all necessary in order to memorize accurately.

Looking for musical patterns in the melody and accompaniment will help organize the music and make memorizing easier. It is a good idea to practice slowly at first and gradually increase the speed until the correct tempo is reached.

When you start memorizing, select pieces that you have learned previously and feel comfortable playing. A favorite piece is a good place to start. There are several senses that should be coordinated when playing from memory:

Touch: Fingering and hand movements.
Hearing: Combined sounds of the melody and accompaniment.
Sight: Visualize the page of music, with special attention to intervals.
Visualize various melody and accompaniment patterns.

Inter-Tribal Prayer (Native American Melody)

Directions: The accompaniment in this piece consists of two patterns that are used repeatedly. They are indicated with brackets in the first two measures. Notice that the melody and accompaniment in the first phrase is the same as in the second phrase. Recognizing similarity in phrases makes learning and memorizing much easier.

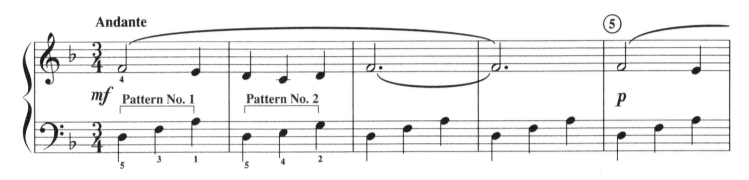

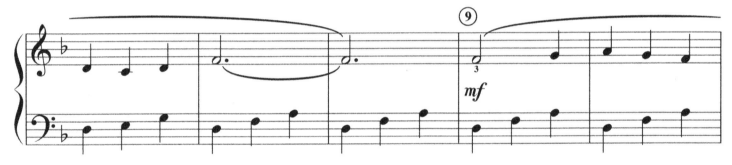

DUET ACCOMPANIMENT

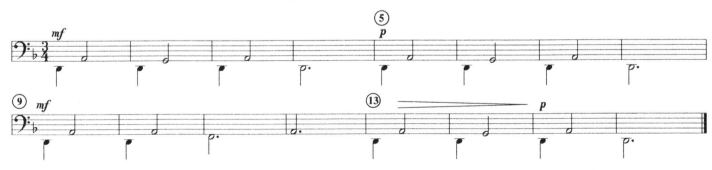

New Note: Treble F
The new note "F" is shown in the sample staff at the right. Refer to the front reference page to find its position on the keyboard.

In the Hall of the Mountain King from "Peer Gynt Suite" (Grieg)

Directions: This piece is in the key of E minor. It is related to the key of G major because both have the same key signature. The new note "F" appears near the end of the piece. The key signature makes it F#.

<u>Reminder:</u> The octave higher sign affects *only the treble clef notes*. All bass clef notes are to be played as written.

Notice that the first six measures of this piece are repeated in the octave-higher section.

Edvard Grieg (GREEG) • 1843-1907 • Norway
Grieg is Norway's best known composer. His fame was spread by the many performances he gave of his own music in other European countries. His wife was a talented singer and often appeared in concerts with him.

Grieg tried to incorporate native Norwegian musical style into his own compositions. He was so successful, that at age 31, the Norwegian government gave him a grant enabling him to spend his time composing.

During 1874-1875 Grieg wrote this piece as part of incidental music to the Ibsen play, "Peer Gynt." The music was later combined into the famous "Peer Gynt Suites." The "Mountain King" is a cave goblin in an old Norwegian fable.

Shenendoah (American Folk Song)

Directions: This piece is in the key of F major. Be sure to play all B's <u>flat</u>.

Watch for places where the thumb crosses under. The lyrics for the first verse are printed between the staffs.

The second and third verses are printed at the bottom of the page.

Oh   Shen - an - doah,____   I   long   to   hear   you,____   Far,   far   a -

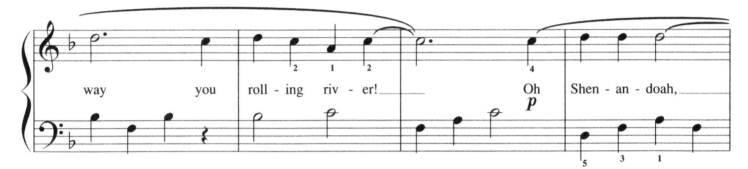

way   you   roll - ing   riv - er!____   Oh   Shen - an - doah,____

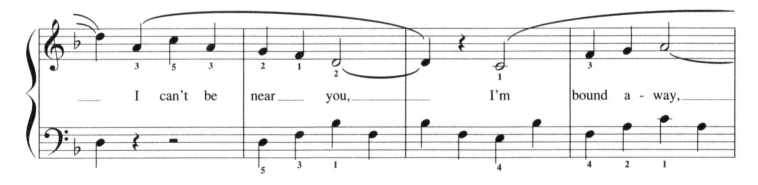

____   I   can't   be   near____   you,____   I'm   bound   a - way,____

____   I'm bound a - way,   A - cross the wide,____   the wide Mis - sour - i.

2. Oh, Shenandoah, I love your daughter,
    Far, far beyond the rolling river!
    She lives across the stormy water
    I'm bound away, I'm bound away.
    Across the wide, the wide Missouri.

3. Oh, Shenandoah, I'm bound to leave you,
    Far, far beyond the rolling river!
    Oh, Shenandoah, I'll not deceive you
    I'm bound away, I'm bound away.
    Across the wide, the wide Missouri.

Musical Form

The planning and structure of music is called its *form*. A **theme** (section of melody) is one of the principal elements of form.

For convenience in analysis, each theme is labeled with a letter. For example, on this page the theme in the first line may be labeled **A**, and the theme in the second line labeled **B**. (These letters have nothing to do with musical notes, but are rather like letters used in an outline.)

When examining the entire piece, you will find that the 1st and 4th lines are the same and the 2nd and 3rd lines are the same. Therefore, the musical form indicating the sequence of themes, may be labeled **A-B-B-A**. Knowing the musical form helps in learning and memorizing a piece of music.

My Sweetheart Is Plowing (Hungarian Peasant Song) (Bartok)*

Directions: Watch for the staccato notes. Although each staccato note is to be released quickly, count carefully in order NOT to play them faster. The correct effect is to make a short gap between each of the staccato notes. The rhythm and tempo should be unchanged.

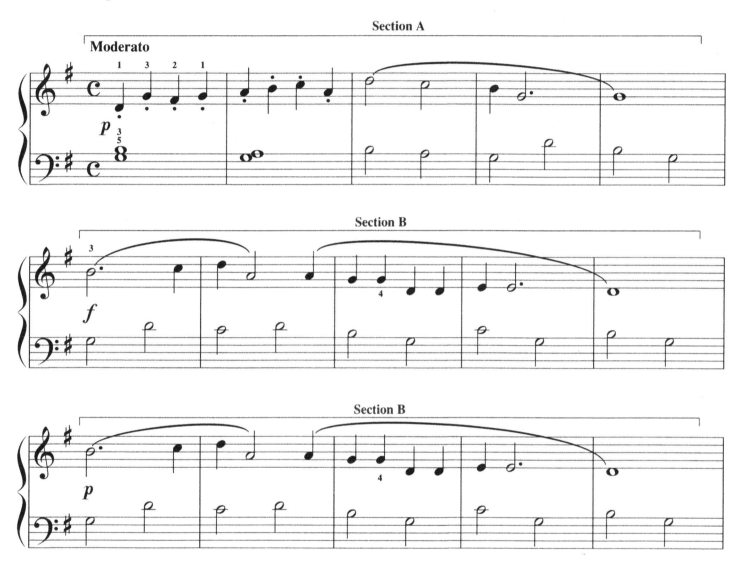

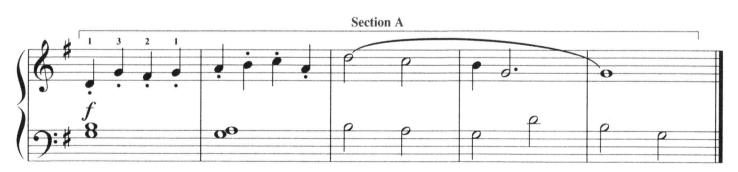

* This song is part of a collection published in 1906. A translation of the lyrics appears here.
    Singing as he plows the land, My sweetheart works all day.
    Clinking clanking, The ox team pulls the plow ahead.
    Tugging, pulling, The soil is dry, the fields are rough.
    Singing as he plows the land, My sweetheart works all day.

New Note: Bass A

The new note "A" is shown in the sample staff at the right. Refer to the front reference page to find its position on the keyboard.

Bacchanale from "Samson and Delila" (Saint-Saens)*

Directions: This piece is in the key of A minor. A minor is related to the key of C major because both have the same key signature.

The bass clef accompaniment consists of just two notes, A and E. They are used in three different rhythmic patterns which are labeled with brackets. These three patterns are alternated and repeated many times.

The tie in measure 11 connects a quarter note to the first of a pair of 8th notes. The counting is printed between staffs.

* "Samson and Delila," based on the Biblical story, was written by Camille Saint-Saens in 1877. It is his best known opera. A "Bacchanale" is a lively, festive party, named after the ancient Roman divinity, Bacchus. The "Bacchanale" is used as a ballet in the last act of the opera. The theme is said to be based on an Oriental melody obtained by Saint-Saens from a Turkish general.

More Musical Form

The musical form (see page 41) of this piece is **A-A¹-B-B¹**. Although the repetitions of the **A** and **B** sections are not identical, there is substantial similarity. Therefore, in the music on this page the second **A** section is labeled **A¹**. The second **B** section is labeled **B¹**.

Put Your Little Foot   (American Folk Dance)

Directions: In the **A** sections, the *rhythm* is the same in both staffs, although the notes are different.

In section **B¹**, one extra note is added to the treble clef melody. Can you find it?

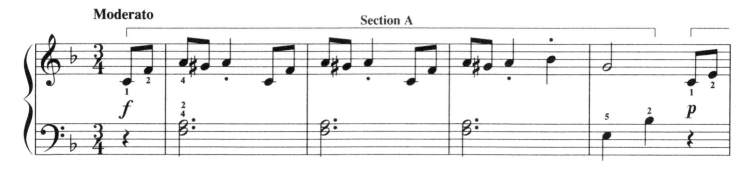

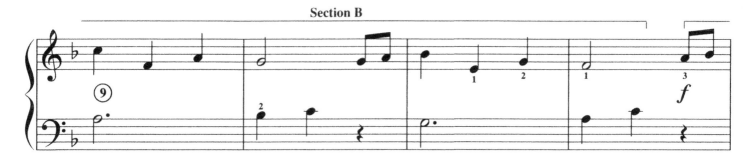

DUET ACCOMPANIMENT

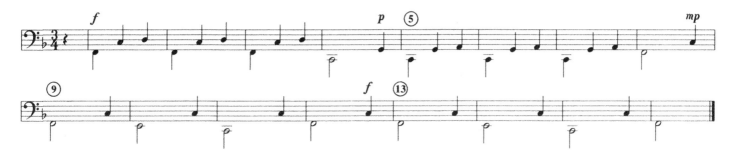

Gypsy Love Song from "The Fortune Teller" (Herbert)

Directions: The two sharps in the key signature indicate the key of D major. Be sure to <u>play all F's and C's sharp</u>. As a preparatory, play each hand separately several times. Watch for the octave lower sign in the final measure.

This piece uses **A-B-A-B¹** form (see page 41). Each line of music represents one letter, for example, the first line is **A** and the second line is **B**, etc. In the final measure, the bass clef is different than in the previous **B** section, therefore, the last line is labeled **B¹**.

Victor Herbert (HER-burt) • 1859-1924 • Ireland

Victor Herbert's family moved from Ireland to Germany when he was 7 years old. He received his musical education in the city of Stuttgart. Shortly after his marriage, he and his wife moved to New York where they both worked for the Metropolitan Opera, he as a cello player and his wife as a singer. He remained in the United States for the rest of his life.

Between 1895 and 1924, Herbert wrote forty operettas which were extremely popular at the time. "The Fortune Teller" was written in 1898.

As a cellist and orchestra conductor, he worked with Thomas Edison in making some of the first recordings of music. Herbert left an important heritage to the music profession by influencing copyright laws and in helping to establish the A.S.C.A.P. (American Society of Composers, Authors and Publishers) which administers royalties for musical performances.

Accompaniment Pattern Analysis
The bass clef accompaniment consists of two chords, F and C, with various rhythms and broken chord patterns. The differing forms of the F chord are shown in the sample measures.

March of the Comedians from "The Bartered Bride" (Smetana)

Directions: This piece uses **A-A¹-B-A²** form. Each line of music is represented by one letter, as on page 44. The second and fourth lines are labeled **A¹** and **A²** because there is a small difference in the last measure of each of these **A** sections.

Bedrich Smetana (SMET-tuh-nah) • 1824-1884 • Bohemia (now part of Czech Republic)
Smetana was the first important composer of Bohemia whose operas helped establish the Czech national opera in Prague. He wrote nine operas, as well as many pieces of orchestral music, chamber muisc, songs and piano solos. He is best known for his comic opera "The Bartered Bride," and a symphonic poem "My Fatherland."

"The Bartered Bride," written and revised several times between 1863 and 1870, brought him international fame. It is a story of love, intrigue, deception and misunderstanding which is all happily resolved. The "March of the Comedians" occurs in Act III, Scene 2, played by a circus band to introduce the performers.

You are now ready to progress to Schaum's PIANO for ADULTS, Level 2.

Reference Page and Music Dictionary - also see Front Inside Cover

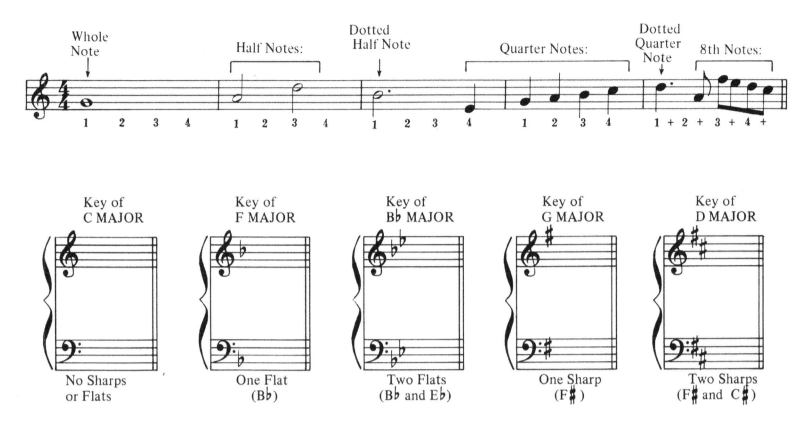

MUSIC DICTIONARY

(Also see Index, page 48)

Most musical terms are Italian, because music writing began in Italy. The accented syllable is shown in *capital* letters.

See the Front Reference Page for illustrations of basic music elements and correlation of notes with their keyboard location.

Terms listed here are limited to those commonly found in Level One methods and supplements.

accent (ACK-sent) Stress or emphasis on a note or chord.

accidental (ack-sih-DEN-tal) Sharp, flat, or natural that does *not* appear in the key signature.

adagio (ah-DAH-jee-o) Slow, slowly.

allegretto (ah-leh-GRET-toh) A little slower than *allegro*.

allegro (ah-LEG-grow) Fast, quickly.

andante (ahn-DAHN-tay) Moderately slow.

animato (ah-nee-MAH-toh) Lively, spirited.

beam Thick line connecting the stems of two or more 8th notes.

chord (KORD) Simultaneous sounding of three or more tones.

common time 4/4 meter. Time signature is: **C**

con brio (kone BREE-oh) With vigor, spirit, or gusto.

cresc. Abbreviation of *crescendo*.

crescendo (cre-SHEN-doh) Gradually increasing in loudness. Also abbreviated with the sign: ⟨

degree Number given to each note of a major or minor scale in ascending sequence.

dim. Abbreviation of *diminuendo*.

diminuendo (di-min-you-END-oh) Becoming gradually less loud. Also abbreviated with the sign: ⟩

dissonance (DISS-uh-nunce) Combination of simultaneous musical sounds that are unpleasant or harsh to the listener.

duet (doo-WHET) Music for two performers.

dynamic marks Same as *expression marks*.

expression marks Signs used to show different levels of loud and soft. For example, *f* and *p*.

extension dot A dot placed to the right of a note head that increases the duration of the note. See page 19.

fermata (ferr-MAH-tah) Hold or wait on a note or chord, longer than its normal duration. Symbol: 𝄐

f Abbreviation of *forte*: loud.

ff Abbreviation of *fortissimo*: very loud.

fine (FEE-nay) End.

flag Short curved line attached to the right side of a stem. A quarter note is changed to an 8th note by adding a flag.

form The organizing and structure of music, usually labeled in outline form, for example, A-A-B-A.

forte (FOHR-tay) Loud, strong. Abbreviation: *f*

fortissimo (fohr-TISS-ee-moh) Very loud. Abbreviation: *ff*

giocoso (jee-oh-KOE-soh) Humorously, playfully.

half step The interval from one key (of a keyboard) to the next closest key, black or white.

interval Distance in sound between one note and another. See page 5.

inversion Regrouping of the notes in an *interval* or *chord*. See page 37.

key signature One or more sharps or flats at the beginning of each staff, next to the clef.

largo (LAHR-goh) Very slow, solemn.

legato (lah-GAH-toh) Notes played in a smooth and connected manner.

leger line (LED-jer) Short horizontal line placed above or below as an extension to the musical staff. Used for writing of individual notes beyond the normal range of the staff. Middle C is written on a leger line. See pages 8 and 36.

L.H. Abbreviation of *left hand.*

lento (LEN-toh) Slow, but not as slow as *largo.*

maestoso (my-ess-TOH-soh) Majestic, dignified, proudly.

major scale A pattern of whole and half steps in the following order: 2-whole steps, one half step, 3-whole steps, and one half step.

metronome (MET-roh-nome) Device to determine tempo or speed in music; measured in beats per minute. The original mechanical metronome was popularized by J.N. Maelzel, therefore the abbreviation, M.M. (Maelzel's metronome).

mezzo forte (MET-zoh FOHR-tay) Medium loud; softer than *forte.* Abbreviation: *mf*

mezzo piano (MET-zoh pee-YAH-noh) Medium soft; louder than *piano.* Abbreviation: *mp*

mf Abbreviation of *mezzo forte:* medium loud.

minor Chord, melody, or scale often having a sad, mysterious, or spooky sound.

misterioso (miss-teer-ee-OH-soh) Mysteriously.

M.M. Abbreviation of Maelzel's metronome. See *metronome.*

moderato (mah-dur-AH-toh) At a moderate tempo or speed.

mp Abbreviation of *mezzo piano:* medium soft.

musical form See *form.*

note head The round part of a musical note.

octave (AHK-tiv) Interval of an 8th; the top and bottom notes have the same letter name.

octave higher sign The number 8, followed by a broken line and placed *above* a series of notes. Indicates notes to be played one octave higher than written. See page 31.

octave lower sign The number 8, followed by a broken line and placed *below* a series of notes. Indicates notes to be played one octave lower than written. See page 31.

op. Abbreviation of *opus.*

opus (OH-puss) Unit of musical work usually numbered in chronological order. May be a composition of any length from a short single piece, a collection of pieces, to a full symphony or opera.

p Abbreviation of *piano:* Soft.

phrase (FRAZE) Group of successive notes dividing a melody or accompaniment pattern into a logical section. This is comparable to the way sentences divide text into sections. See page 6.

phrase mark Curved line, placed over or under groups of notes, indicating the length of a phrase. The notes of a phrase are usually played *legato.* See page 6.

pianissimo (pee-ah-NISS-ee-moh) Very soft. Abbreviation: *pp*

piano (pee-YAA-noh) Soft. Abbreviation: *p*

pianoforte (pee-yaa-noh-FOR-tay) Original full name for the *piano,* chosen because it was the first keyboard instrument to effectively play in a wide range of dynamics; thus the combination of words *piano* and *forte* (literally: soft-loud).

pick up One or more notes, at the beginning of a piece which are less than a complete measure. Often called *up-beat notes.*

pp Abbreviation of *pianissimo:* Very soft.

repertoire (reh-per-TWAR) Musical compositions previously studied, mastered, and currently maintained by a musician or musical group so that performance can be given with a minimum of preparation.

rest A symbol for silence placed in the staff. A rest shows where and how long NO note is to sound.

R.H. Abbreviation of *right hand.*

rit. Abbreviation of *ritardando.*

ritard. Abbreviation of *ritardando.*

ritardando (ree-tahr-DAHN-doh) Gradually getting slower in tempo.

root 1) Key note of a chord, the same as the letter name of a chord symbol. 2) Lowest note of a root position chord.

root position The position of a triad or chord in which the *root* note is on the bottom and the other notes are stacked above.

scale Sequence of musical tones collectively forming a key or tonality, usually named after the starting tone. See page 16-17.

scale passage Portion of a scale. See page 18.

semplice (SEMM-plee-chay) Simple, plain.

slur Curved line, placed over or under groups of notes indicating *legato.* Often the same as a *phrase mark.*

staccato (stah-KAH-toh) Short, detached, separated. Indicated by a dot *above or below* a note head. See page 19.

staff Group of five horizontal lines used for note placement.

stem Vertical line attached to a note head.

step The distance from one musical letter to the very next letter.

tempo (TEMM-poh) Rate of speed used for musical beats or meter.

tempo di marcia (TEMM-poh dih MAHR-chee-ah) March time.

tempo mark Word or words at the beginning of a piece of music explaining the rate of speed to be used. For example, *allegro, andante, moderato.*

tie Curved line that connects two notes on the same line or space that are next to each other. The values of the tied notes are added together joining into one continuous sound. See pages 6 and 37.

time signature Two large numbers, above each other in the staff, at the beginning of a piece of music. The *upper* number tells how many counting numbers or beats are in each measure. The *lower* number tells which kind of note gets one counting number. If the lower number is 4, the *quarter note* gets one counting number.

tonic (TAHN-ik) Starting note or first degree of a scale.

transpose (trans-POZE) To play a melody or chord in a different key, starting on a higher or lower note. When transposing, a different key signature and hand position are used. See pages 14 and 15.

triad (TRY-add) Chord with three notes.

upbeat (UP-beet) See *pick up notes.*

vivace (vee-VAH-chay) Lively, quick.

vivo (VEE-voh) Lively, animated.

whole step The distance from one key (on the keyboard) to another with *one key in between* (black or white). The same as two *half steps.* See pages 12 and 13.

Index